One day in Medieval England

DAY BOOK SERIES

Acknowledgements

We should like to express our gratitude to all those who have kindly
granted copyright permission for photographs in this volume, and special
thanks to our illustrators.

The Trustees of the British Museum: pages 17, 20, 21 (top), 28 (bottom), 29, 32 (top)

The Trustees of the London Museum: pages 26 (bottom), 34 (bottom), 35, 36 (top), 37, 40 (bottom left)

The Mansell Collection: pages 4, 7, 8, 9, 10, 11, 12, 13, 14, 15, 16, 18 (bottom), 19, 21 (bottom), 22, 26 (top), 27, 28 (top), 30, 31 (top), 32 (bottom), 33, 34 (top), 36 (bottom), 38, 39, 40 (top and bottom right), 41

Rosemary Holliday: illustration, page 42

Brian Lewis: illustrations, pages 5, 24–25

Cecilia Ware: line drawings and illustration, pages 18 (top), 23, 31 (bottom)

© 1974 ROBERT TYNDALL LTD.

All Rights Reserved. No part of this publication may be reproduced, stored in a
retrieval system, or transmitted in any form or by any means, electronic, mechanical, photocopying, recording or otherwise, without the prior permission of the
Copyright owner.

ISBN 85949 058 0

Printed by Page Bros (Norwich) Ltd., Norwich, England

One day in Medieval England

by Michael Hobbs

TYNDALL

Opposite page, left to right:
Sir Edmund of Lampwich,
Lady Anne, William Palmer,
Meg Palmer,
Abbot Hubert, Tom Palmer,
Jack of Newbury

One of the earliest detailed maps of Great Britain

Contents

Introduction	6
MORNING	7
AFTERNOON	23
EVENING	34
Glossary	43
General Notes	45
Index	47
Further Reading	48

AD 1370

Introduction

The medieval ballads of 'courtly love' give an idealised impression of life at that time. For the ordinary people of England, in the service of the lord of the manor, life was often hard. Churchmen and aristocracy lived in a style far removed from that of the common man.

History is fun; but a list of unconnected accounts of battles and events is not.

History is the story of how we, the human race, governed, fought, learned and lived in years gone by. The influence of one people upon another, and often of one man upon a nation, is crucial to the development of civilisation.

In this series, we look at the customs and events of an age, and history is shown through the eyes of those who were living at the time.

The series is intended as an introduction to a period, and great care has been taken to see that all illustrations, photographs and artwork are accurate. Where an illustration is not specifically from the year in which the book is set, the caption explains its relevance and, wherever possible, its date.

Words in italics in the text (italicised only at their first appearance) are explained in the Glossary, and there is further information on some aspects of the times in the General Notes. An Index is provided for easy reference, but it is recommended that the book be read as a whole to begin with.

Having had a taste of the atmosphere of the age, you may be interested to read more about some of the people, their homes, politics, literature, society, religious beliefs and customs. There is a Further Reading list at the back of the book, but this represents only a small number of the many books available. Have a look in your library and see what you can find.

Left: The Abbey and cloisters of a Benedictine monastery. Below: A Benedictine monk

MORNING

As usual Abbot Hubert woke at midnight and rose from his hard *pallet* without regret. Less happily he put on his *hair shirt* and the black gown of his *Benedictine* order and made his way down cold stairs and corridors, through the abbey *cloisters* to the chapel where his monks had already gathered from their dormitories to celebrate *Matins* and *Lauds*.

He found the religious discipline of his order hard, but had to set an example to the monks in his charge and so he too participated in the manual labour; St. Benedict had decreed that this was good for the soul when he set up the monastery of *Monte Cassino* eight hundred years earlier. Abbot Hubert obeyed every tolling of the abbey bell that marked the divisions of the day. True, the manual labour allotted to him was not the hard work that many monks were obliged to do. He helped to tend the herb gardens for a few hours each week, and for many years had spent an equal amount of time each week in the *scriptorium* making a beautifully illuminated copy of the Old Testament. This was a labour of love; Hubert had taken pleasure in the beauties of fine manuscripts ever since he had first learnt to write as a young monk.

7

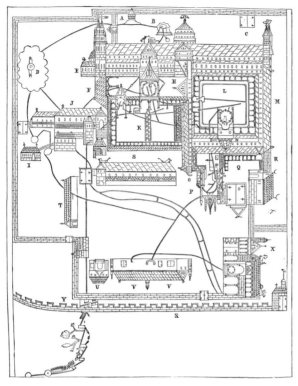

Plan in relief of a 12th century Benedictine Priory at Canterbury. (A) belfry; (B) fountain; (C) cemetery; (D) reservoir, with conduit pipes; (E) Canterbury Cathedral; (F) vestry; (G) crypt; (H) chapter-house; (I) prior's house; (J) infirmary and annexes; (K) kitchen garden with well, pumps and water pipes; (L) cloister; (M) cellar; (N) dormitory; (O) refectory; (P) kitchens; (Q) parlour; (R) house for the guests and the poor; (S) water-closets; (T) baths; (U) granary; (V) bakehouse and brewery; (X) the chief entrance; (Y, Z) fortified wall of the Abbey and the city

As he made his way back to his cell, after his religious duties were completed, he wished that he had more time to spend on such work; but the young monk had become a man of business with the passing of the years. As head of the Abbey he was in charge of one of the largest estates in England. His Abbey owned more lands than all save the most powerful nobles of the realm, and its business was more diverse and reached further over the seas than that of many merchants of London, Bristol and Exeter.

The Abbey owned twenty-two manors as well as the 1,500 acres that surrounded St. Bartholomew's Abbey itself, and it was Hubert's task to administer it well and see that every activity made a good profit. The Abbey had a range of activities as wide as any town or any powerful lord's estate in the country. Outside there were orchards, vineyards, meadows, vast open fields, herb, fruit and vegetable gardens and fish ponds. All had to be kept well stocked. There was also open heathland where sheep, pigs and goats wandered. Many of these animals belonged to *cottars* and *villeins* who owed similar duties to the Abbot as the villagers of nearby Lampwich owed to Sir Edmund, the lord of the manor.

The Abbey buildings were many and were reminiscent of a very large and prosperous Roman farming villa. There were breweries, wineries, butteries, dairies, laundries, libraries, baking houses, guest houses, workshops for carpentry, binding, making clothes and metalwork, and of course the kitchens – forgetting the original severe rules set down by St. Benedict, most monks ate very well indeed. They were also as well equipped as the Roman villas of a thousand years earlier, with drains, water pipes, bath houses and even lavatories. The same cannot be said of a medieval lord's manor house or castle; in comparison, despite the splendid tapestries, brilliant clothing, fine jewellery and silver and gold tableware, these latter were very unhealthy places to live in – cold and draughty, dirty and with very little sanitation.

When Abbot Hubert awoke later with the new dawn, he thought of his humble beginnings and how he now ruled over a farming and trading empire. He was the son of a peasant, who had looked about him and realised that almost

8

the only way for a young man of poor family to make his way in the world was to join the Church. Not as a village parson however, for many of these were as poor as their flock, but any lad, if he was intelligent and worked hard, had a chance in a monastic order. Hubert's father had heard too how some men, having learnt to read and write, and keep accounts, and having studied the law, had become great men in England. This had been the route to power of *St. Thomas à Becket* who had risen to be *Henry II's* Chancellor, and therefore the most powerful man, and one of the richest, in the country, before Henry made him *Archbishop of Canterbury.*

Hubert knew he had fulfilled all his father's hopes for him, but he himself often wished he could lay down his burdens and return to the life of a poor monk that he had led during his early years at St. Bartholomew's. However his heart lightened when he remembered that today was to be different. Sir Edmund of Lampwich had called the previous morning to pay his respects on his return from the Holy Land, and Hubert was bidden to join an afternoon's hunting and the ensuing feast. Probably he would not eat as well as at the Abbey and the woods and *coverts* would not be so well stocked, but it would be pleasant to get away from his everyday cares and the sometimes critical eyes of monks who thought they were holier than he was.

Orders had been given the day before and he would set out shortly with some men-at-arms, drawn from the Abbey's tenants, who were bound to follow him to war or on business and pleasure trips. While he was away his fellow monks would complain that he thought more of his business and pleasure than of God, but Hubert felt he was doing God's work by increasing the wealth of the Church and his own Abbey. At least he had nothing to do with the selling of pardons to sinners who thought they could buy God's forgiveness from a *pardoner* or a passing friar. As Hubert rode out he had a clear conscience.

Tom Palmer stirred as the first dawn light glowed through the oiled linen-cloth of the window. Elsewhere in the room no one moved yet. A stiff stalk of straw, disturbed by Tom's movement, was now piercing through his gown and worry-

Above: The murder of Thomas à Becket in Canterbury Cathedral, from a medieval manuscript.
Below: Illustration of the Pardoner from Chaucer's 'Canterbury Tales', taken from the Ellesmere Manuscript

9

Right: Medieval village scene showing the many uses to which cereal crops were put, such as bread-making, roof-thatching and fencing

Below: Impression of a peasant, drawn by a contemporary artist

ing at the sensitive flesh around his shoulder blade; but Tom was used to the discomforts of a straw bed and slept on. By now the outline of the room was becoming clear: it had an earth floor, a thatched roof above, and three walls constructed of roughly-hewn logs. The fourth wall had been rebuilt after flood waters from the manor stream had scoured underneath the upright logs and swept them away, when the snows had melted that spring. The family had rebuilt it, using upright beams with an infilling of stone rubble bonded together with clay. The new wall kept the wind out much better than the old one and the family now slept against it.

In the centre of the room the last remnant of a fire smouldered and a few wisps of smoke spiralled upwards and away through the uncovered windows. Tom's father William was always talking of building a chimney but no one in the village knew how to do the job. It would have to wait until a travelling *mason* passed their way.

The bird song, followed soon by the crowing of a cockerel nearby, together with the dawn light and the troublesome straw stalk, finally brought Tom to wakefulness. He sat up, scratching busily at head and body because of the

10

irritation of the lice and fleas. His father and mother still slept – probably more comfortable than he on their bed of flock bags. He made his way out through the back of the house to the well, which was in the middle of a patch of ground where they grew enough vegetables for their own use, and he drew up an oak bucket of water. He did not wash very thoroughly because this was widely thought to be weakening; he merely swished the sleep from his eyes and splashed his face. He had heard that some lords and ladies were taking to a new fashion of bathing but that was all right for them: they did not need the strength to work all day in the fields.

By this time his father William and Meg, his mother, were also awake and preparing for the new day. William was feeling that it was going to bring trouble. He was the *reeve* of the manor. The law was that villeins of a lord had the right to elect a reeve who would act as a middleman between the villagers and the manor, and who would help to organize the work. Like most lords, Sir Edmund had ignored the rule and had himself appointed William, probably for life, just before he had left on the last *Crusade* of *Peter of Cyprus.* Although the job meant that his family had more to live on than the rest of the ordinary villagers, William often wondered if the worries that went with it were quite worth the extra money. His friends criticised him for carrying out the orders of the manor.

It was a time of great unrest amongst labourers all over England. For centuries they had believed that they were born to their dreary way of life and that nothing could be altered, just as if the lord of the manor were God and his word the law. The *Black Death* had changed all that. Men were still willing to accept the power of the king but increasingly muttered against the power and wealth of lords and abbots. Some wandering priests even preached that all men were equal and there was a saying heard on many lips:

When Adam *delved* and Eve span
Who was then a gentleman?

William was not sure whether or not he agreed with its meaning that at the Creation there were no lords and ladies

Above: A draw-well probably of the sort that Tom used. **Below:** A reeve – the man responsible for organizing the work on the lord's demesne

The Black Death was one of the worst forms of plague. The epidemics caused widespread suffering and fear in all sections of society. The last great plague infested London as late as the 17th century

or even gentlemen, and that everyone really was born equal. Things had certainly changed since then.

He wondered, as he got dressed, if he would be able to find enough workers to gather in Sir Edmund's crops. So many people had died in the Black Death that there were no longer enough people to work the land. So labourers and craftsmen had asked for more money. Wages for a while had gone up to absurd heights – Will the ploughman had even asked for 40s (the equivalent of about £140 today) a year. The law that had been passed to keep wages down to what they had been before the Black Death only made everyone discontented and if one lord would not pay what was asked, a worker would slip away and find another who would. Although the law forbade a worker to move like this and branded him for doing so, there was no police force or sure system to track the man down and bring him back again. So a lord had to break the law and pay what was asked or see his land going to waste and his crops rotting in the fields.

The workers that William Palmer was in charge of had other reasons to be angry nowadays as well. Sir Edmund and his father before him had allowed some of his rights over the peasants to lapse but the Lady Anne had brought them back into use again when Sir Edmund had been captured by the *Saracens*, and she had to raise the money for a *ransom*. The bringing back of certain taxes had caused quite a stir. There was *merchet* for example, a fine that had to be paid to the lord when a daughter got married – and a son too, sometimes – and *heriot*, which meant that when a villein died, the lord took his best animal or possession. The Lady Anne had also ordered the wives to stop baking their own bread and to use the oven at the manor, and the men had to grind their corn at the manor mill – in both cases, of course, they were charged for doing so.

Some of these were things that did not happen often to a family, but it was the return of another custom which caused the most anger. In the past a villein had had to work so many days a week on his lord's land without payment. Over the years this custom had gradually seemed to be fading away all over England but with the rise in wages some lords had asserted their right to unpaid work again. Lady Anne, desperate for money – money for fine clothes and furniture as well as to pay the ransom for Sir Edmund –

A Saracen warrior from an Arabian manuscript

Left: An example of the type of corn hand-mill that would have been used on Sir Edmund's manor

13

A 14th century lady with her lady-in-waiting

had brought the custom back. William had found that the returned custom had not done much good. The men might be working for nothing but as they were angry they did not work well. The days of slavery in England had gone, though some lords seemed not to realise it.

William had tried to explain the trouble that had been caused by Lady Anne's changes to the way things were done, but she had refused to pay him any attention, saying only that God had set kings and lords over the common people and that labourers must work and sweat, and be grateful that they were ever paid any money at all. He was not surprised when some cows and sheep had been found with their hamstrings cut the day before. It had probably been done out of revenge by a worker – someone who would perhaps have been content enough if the old customs had not been brought back by Lady Anne. Perhaps Sir Edmund, when he got back from the dungeon of a Saracen castle, would be more sensible.

It did not pay to have a woman running things, in William's opinion, at least not one as young as Lady Anne, left by her lord so soon after their marriage, and before she had had time to see how a manor was run. It had not helped either that she was unable to read or write. Neither

Right: Originally a Saracen stronghold, this castle was seized by the French in the 12th century. It was then rebuilt and became the fortress of the Knights Hospitallers. **Below:** A dungeon

14

could Sir Edmund but at least his father and the *bailiff* had shown him how a manor should be run when he was a lad. Certainly if Sir Edmund would not listen to reason there would be more trouble.

William had heard of riots against lords and abbots in various parts of the country and he feared that the same thing could happen in Lampwich. And once again he would find himself in the middle between his lord and the villagers, many of whom he thought of as his friends. He decided to go up to the manor, see Lady Anne and perhaps, over a discussion about the accounts, he might be able to make her see some sense. Perhaps the business of the cut hamstrings would persuade her. She should be able to see that a farm just cannot be run if the workers really decide to cause trouble. There were things a man could do to crops as well as animals so that the wheat and barley might rot in the barn, the seed fail to *germinate*; there was one labourer who had broken three ploughs already that year 'accidentally' since he had once more been forced to plough sixteen days a year without payment, on the manor lands.

Tom burst in, his hair still tangled and dripping from its dousing at the well. In great excitement he told them that it was all over the village that Sir Edmund was back. Accompanied by his *squire* Robert, he had run down the village drunk who was on his staggering way home from the ale house. The drunk had got a broken leg out of the sudden meeting in the darkness, and a *groat* for his pain, but news to tell that was making him an important man that morning.

William was pleased. He would find Sir Edmund easier to deal with and perhaps more sensible now that he had got that nonsense about crusading to save Jerusalem and the Holy Land out of his head. And there would be celebrations too. There was nothing like a fight, a visit of *mummers* to act out scenes from the Bible in the church porch or, best of all, a feast to stop the menfolk complaining. Sir Edmund had the chance to begin again and if he took William's advice they might all avoid more trouble.

Tom in fact had news of the feast and of other things besides. Sir Edmund and the Lady Anne were to go hunting in the early afternoon. Messages had already been sent

Crusading knights enter the city they have just captured

An Edward III groat, showing obverse and reverse

Falconers training their birds

German tapestry showing peasants at work on the land

out through the surrounding area bidding lords and ladies to the hunt and the feasting of the evening. Sir Edmund had apparently returned very late during the night because he had paused here and there the previous day to invite and drink with the friends he had not seen for so long.

Today was to be quite an occasion and there was one thing in particular that was exciting Tom. The *falconer* had died a few months before, after teaching Tom the tricks and skills of his trade. Tom had shown an aptitude for the business and had enjoyed the work of months required to get a *peregrine* to trust its handler, fly to and return from a lure and, in the end, soar up seeking its prey and return to the thickly-gauntleted hand after it had plummeted down and sunk its talons into rabbit, hare or partridge. Once he had stayed with a falcon in the smoky, dim rushlight through a night and a day and well on into the following night, keeping awake himself as the bird glared unblinkingly at him; but he had won. In the end the bird's eyes had closed in sleep. It had admitted that it trusted him enough to sleep in his presence. Then he had been able to begin the job of training it to know what each command meant and to obey him. Now he would almost certainly be able to use his skills in the hunt.

Tom was excited about the feast too. William was pleased to hear that Sir Edmund was making a good start. As well as the nobles of the vicinity he was also inviting the villagers. Not everyone of course, but all those who rented land from him or had raised themselves just a little above the level of a cottar or *bordar*. William would be at the feast too, and so would his wife and son, though they would have to work for their supper – Meg in the kitchens and Tom to serve the noble guests.

However, there was work to do in plenty before that. William reminded Tom that there was hoeing to be done on Sir Edmund's strips in the Great Field. If he worked until eleven o'clock before seeing to his falcons in the hunt, William would have a word with the bailiff so that Tom was credited with a full day's labour. Now he must make his way to the manor to find out what his tasks were to be on this important day, while Tom made his way, hoe in hand, to the beans.

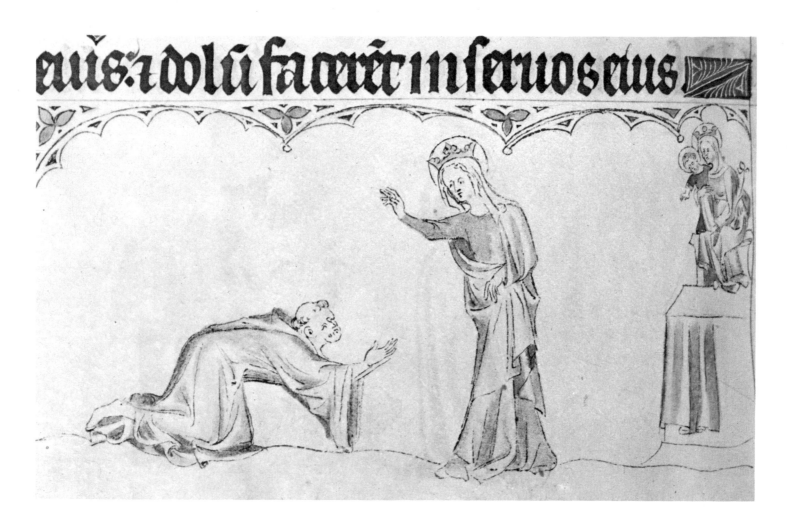

Something sharper than a straw stalk had woken Jack of Newbury – a pitchfork. He had not wanted to spend the money on a night's lodging at an inn, and when he had asked for shelter at St. Bartholomew's Abbey they had threatened to set the hunting dogs on him. Jack felt it was unfair that so many people thought a *pedlar* was a thief. Although he was willing to sell a *pig in a poke* and exaggerated the quality and splendour of the trinkets, pots and cloth that he had to sell, he had never actually stolen.

Nevertheless he had had to bed down for the night with his donkey, in the corner of a barn at St. Bartholomew's and it was a monk's pitchfork that had stung him awake. The thought passed through Jack's mind that it was a pity he had forgotten how early such people always awoke to say their prayers.

Medieval manuscript illuminations. **Above:** An Abbess blesses a monk after confession. To the right of the picture is an altar with a statue of the Madonna and Child. **Below:** Portrayal of a Benedictine Abbot with mitre and crook

17

A sower, from a medieval manuscript

This illustration shows agricultural tasks at all seasons of the year; digging ditches, planting trees, ploughing, harrowing, sowing, weeding, hoeing, 'weaving hedges', reaping and winnowing

Quickly he explained that he had travelled far the day before and when it was dark had stumbled, lost, upon the barn. The monk, however, did not seem to have the usual prejudice against pedlars and had prodded him only to wake him up and question him. Jack explained that he was a travelling salesman, and he asked the way to the nearest village; he was told that Lampwich lay about eight miles off and that he would pass some isolated hamlets along the way where he might make a sale or two. The day had not begun so badly for Jack after all, and before he went on his way he had sold the monk a new razor for his *tonsure*.

The landscape through which Tom walked to the fields was very different from the way it is today. Although modern farmers are gradually doing away with the dry-stone walls, fences and hedges that divide one field from another so that larger and larger farm machinery has more room to manoeuvre, the English countryside seen from a bird's-eye view or a hilltop is still a patchwork of fields of green, brown and honey. Medieval farmland was very different in appearance.

Lampwich Manor had three fields, each of about 250 acres and each with a temporary fence thrown up around the crops during the summer to keep animals away. The fields were divided up into a large number of strips, marked off from each other by the mound that the plough threw up. A strip was about 220 yards long, a *furlong*, about as far as a team of eight oxen could heave a wooden plough before pausing for rest. Each of the villagers had a number of strips to cultivate for his own needs or profit. William Palmer had 14 strips and was quite well off. To keep some goodness in the land different crops were grown each year, and at Lampwich and many other manors one of the fields lay *fallow* for one whole year in every three. No one really knew why this was good for the land but experience had proved that it was.

The crops that Tom and the villagers grew are still common in English farming today. Nevertheless, there were some very important absentees. Tom was used to seeing wheat, rye, oats, barley, peas and *vetches* in the fields, but not root crops such as potatoes – which, like tobacco,

18

were first seen in England in Elizabethan times – nor swedes, turnips and beets. This meant that few cattle and pigs could be kept through the winter because there was not enough food to feed them. All but a few were slaughtered at the end of the summer when the supply of grass began to fail; the few that were kept would be used for breeding in the following spring. The hardier sheep were a different matter of course: they would remain outside in cold weather and were able to find just about enough to exist on through the winter.

The lord's land, called his *demesne*, was kept separate from that of the villagers for the most part, and so was the *glebe* which belonged to the village parson. Their animals, however, were kept in common with those of their tenants and other villagers – and a poor lot to modern eyes they were. At this time no attempt was made at *selective breeding*, and it meant that hereditary diseases were passed down through the stock; animals of poor quality were bred with the better ones so that there was never any improvement in the herds.

Laboriously Tom made his way along each furrow, hoeing out the smaller weeds and using a tool with a prong at the end to grasp at the base of the larger weeds and a stout stick with a broad bottom, with which he pressed against the other prong. Once the weed was grasped in this way he could pull it from the soil with a quick jerk.

So the long morning passed as the sun rose towards its full height, and when Tom judged that it was about 11 o'clock he went home for lunch.

The sun had long been slanting through the high-set windows with their expensive glass, and Tom Palmer and his family and Jack the pedlar had been up well before the Lady Anne stirred. For her there was no coarse bedding to hustle her to wakefulness. Her limbs were comforted by the good quality linen that she wished could be exchanged for silk. More tired than usual by the talk and not a little drinking of the night before to greet her husband back from the Crusades, she slept on and on until well past 9 o'clock. Beside her, Sir Edmund – she had forgotten to water his wine – snored and slept with the smile on his lips of one

The above shows the type of hoe that Tom used to clear the weeds from each furrow

The interior of a 14th century bedroom showing the large bed, probably similar to the one in which Lady Anne slept

19

Illustrations taken from medieval manuscripts.
Above: A lord places a ring on his lady's finger.
Below: Knights tilting at each other with lances

who has made his peace with life, God and good red wine.

Lady Anne looked at him without affection. Was it right that parents could tell their daughters whom they must marry? Anne remembered the strong, handsome young squire that her father had been training for knighthood at her childhood home. Her father had been very angry when he had come upon the squire singing her some French nonsense of a ballad. How tenderly the young man had looked at her when the words spoke of a young squire riding away to win plunder in war and coming back to claim the hand of his lady. Her father had put a stop to that very quickly indeed. He had not realised before, for lords and ladies saw little of their children in medieval times, that his daughter was fourteen and had been of marriageable age for some time. Something must be done about it and quickly.

The husband beside her now was the result of a bargain in which she had been the only loser. In the space of a few weeks she was married to a man she had never seen before. No one had thought to tell her Sir Edmund was forty-five

20

tatis: qui fingis laborem in precepto.
Captabunt in animam iusti: et san
guinem innocentem condempnabunt.

either, though something like this was always to be expected. Then there had come his dream telling him to go on
Crusade and, as he began to sell off land and even the household plate, she had realised what a bad bargain her parents
had made. So much in haste had her father been that he
had failed to find her a wealthy husband.

Then she had been alone, entrusted with the running of
the estate and the giving of orders to servants, overseers,
villeins and serfs who were all far older than she was. Still,
she had managed and the estate had even prospered until
the recent troubles. When Sir Edmund had been captured
in Syria she had even succeeded in raising the ransom for
his release; but news and people travelled slowly between
England and *Outremer*. Five years had passed since her
wedding day.

She must get up. People would think it very odd if she
were not busy with the celebrations for her husband's
return; it might cause them to gossip about the young
knight who had once been a squire at her father's manor

Above: From the Luttrell Psalter manuscript,
peasants ploughing with oxen. **Below:** At a royal
marriage the ring was placed on the second finger
of the right hand

A stylized representation of a group of
people warming themselves before the
large fire in the Great Hall. Note that
the whole of the chimney has been
drawn, even to the stork's nest
perched on the top

Illustration from a German
manuscript showing falconers outside
a castle, about to exercise their birds

and who often rode over to accompany her for a day's
hunting . . . There was much to be done and many
orders to give for the day's hunting, and then the feast in
the evening to which she would have to invite many of the
village folk. Later she would be able to hold a longer
celebration just for her relatives and her neighbours from
the surrounding manors.

She dressed, descended to the Great Hall and summoned
the reeve and huntsman. William Palmer soon arrived
and was put in charge of the whole affair, for the huntsman
had been thrown from his horse the day before and was not
fit to ride. William now advised his mistress of the route the
hunt should take and where on the estate were the most
likely places for the hounds to come upon the scent of a
stag. Failing a stag, there must be the chance of a hare or
two but they had to avoid the parts where foxes might be, as
it was difficult to prevent the dogs going after this kind of
vermin, thus wasting a good day's hunting.

They parted. The Lady Anne went to the kitchen to give
instructions for the feast, and William to dine at his home
and to tell young Tom that he would now definitely be
falconer at the hunt. As the lad had trained a couple of
peregrines in the past year he should be able to manage
well enough.

The Palmers had begun their meal before William's return
as they thought he might be given something in the kitchens
as was usual when he had duties at the manor. Tom ate
hurriedly but with appetite. He must go up to the manor to
exercise the falcons but not feed them or they would have
little zest for hunting.

There was not much to eat that morning: it was between
seasons and the glut of early summer was past, but it was
not yet time to kill off stock to save winter feed. However,
though the Lady Anne was well known for her meanness,
there would have to be ample to eat that evening. It would
be an insult to the return of her lord otherwise. The family
made do on the remains of a lark pie, made from the birds
Tom had netted a couple of days before, and some cold
cabbage and salt bacon – all washed down with a mild
beer made without hops.

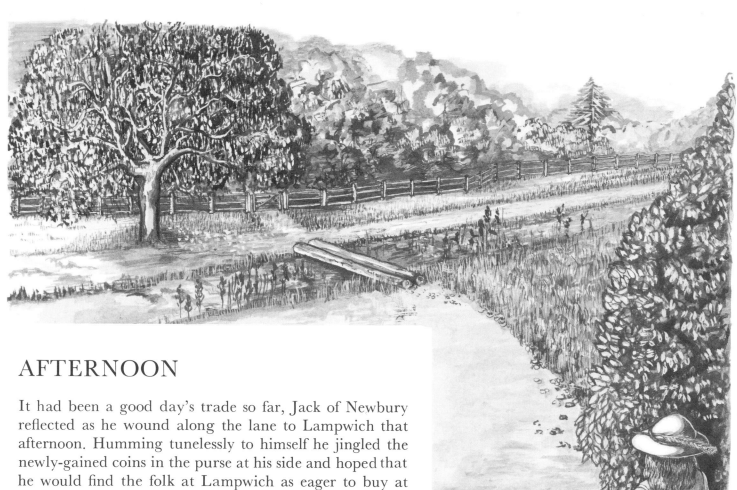

AFTERNOON

It had been a good day's trade so far, Jack of Newbury reflected as he wound along the lane to Lampwich that afternoon. Humming tunelessly to himself he jingled the newly-gained coins in the purse at his side and hoped that he would find the folk at Lampwich as eager to buy at high prices – and sell at low the things he could later sell somewhere else. Clouds of dust rose up as Jack and his donkey plodded steadily through the early afternoon along the rutted country lane, now several inches deep in drifted dusty soil, that would become an almost impassable mire immediately any rain fell.

Carefully he led his donkey across the two rough-hewn tree trunks which bridged the stream; it carried very little water now after the long dry spell. As he rounded a bend where the track curved to follow the bank of the stream, the little cluster of dwellings that was Lampwich came into view. Jack paused. He must smarten himself up and check his wares before entering the place. He would be selling to the womenfolk and, although he would as usual depend on his quick tongue in praising the excellence of his wares, he had long found that a woman bought more readily from a

smart-looking rogue than a dull honest one. So he straightened his *hose*, patted the dust from his *doublet* and felt along the line of his jaw. Good, he did not need a shave yet: he could last another day or so before the blonde bristles would really need scraping. Now for his *panniers*. From the depths of one of these deep baskets he began to take out a multitude of brightly coloured lengths of cloth and linen. The dust from his travels must be shaken out and everything refolded so that there would be nothing amiss which might turn an eager purchaser into a doubtful one. Some of the materials had changed hands several times by *barter* and sale and needed careful folding so that stains would not be noticed.

The contents of another pannier then received similar treatment. Caps, hats, girdles, gloves, *kerchiefs*, hose were all shaken out and neatly refolded and stowed away again. The remainder of the goods he had to sell were mostly hardware requiring much less careful treatment – only a quick polish here and there to a pewter pot or plate, and a quick check through to see that everything would come easily to hand when his quick eyes saw a lack that his wares could fill.

25

In this early 14th century illustration, a lady with a small dog inspects the pedlar's wares hung up outside her door

At last he was satisfied. With a final twitch at his cap and an open honest look on his face, he entered Lampwich, hindered only by a dog which snarled at his heels. Seeing that his approach had not been observed, he ridded himself of that nuisance by a sudden and savage blow with his staff which sent it whimpering into the ditch.

He began to call out the wonder and the usefulness of his wares and it was not long before his calls brought the women to their doors. To them he was a world apart from their everyday lives in which their interests were tied to what happened to their lord in his manor and the eighty or so people of the village. Perhaps once a year they might walk the three miles to the nearest village for a birth, a marriage or a death. A visit to a town market or fair was for the menfolk and even then only for those who had business there or a job to do for the lord or his bailiff. To these women Jack was more than a mere pedlar of wares. He was also the bringer of news and stories from the world outside. It was easy selling to people so grateful for the stories he had to tell them.

Right: An embroidered purse of the 13th or 14th century

26

He could stop his calls now. The people knew he was here and their curiosity would bring them to him. Not looking at the villagers any more he began to spread out his wares, taking care to unfurl the cloths and linens in a broad sweep through the air so that the bright colours caught the eye. Dented and dull as much of his pewterware was, he nevertheless placed each article on the ground with a reverence more fitted to silver goblets for a lord's table.

He now had an audience of some twenty women and, though he still seemed lost in concentration on setting out the things he had to sell, his eyes darted around, taking in those details of appearance that gave the clue to a possible sale. A woman without a kerchief, or with her hose a network of holes, was a buyer if she had a coin or two or something to barter.

Nevertheless there was something different in the air today. Already, before he had even finished setting out his enticing wares, the women were paying him no attention at all. Lively and excited talk had broken out among them. Quietening his irritation that the show he was putting on made so little impression on the women, he listened to the hubbub and was able to pick out a word here and there.

The village, it seemed, had news of its own today. Late last night Sir Edmund had returned from Outremer. Jack was surprised; the great days of the Crusades when kings had ridden with hosts of knights, priests and the common people to the Holy Land were long past. Jerusalem had been won for Christianity and lost again; Norman knights had carved out new *fiefs* for themselves in Syria and Palestine and these too had passed back into the hands of the Saracens. Throughout the Middle East the Christians who had won new lands for themselves had been swept out by the rebirth of *Moslem* military power. No longer were the appeals of the Pope of any avail when he declared that it was the duty of all good Christians to fight so that the Holy Places of the Christian religion in Jerusalem and elsewhere in Palestine should be in Christian hands. The pure religious devotion that had brought about the first Crusade had quickly subsided, so that men soon journeyed to fight in the Holy Land only if they had little of value to leave behind; the East had once been a place where a

Above: Illustration from an old manuscript showing a servant carrying a teapot and platter

Below: The battle with the Saracens for Ascalon during the first Crusade which lasted from 1096–1099

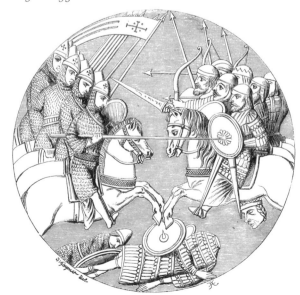

27

Above: Knights of the Holy Ghost make preparations for their voyage, from a miniature in a 14th century manuscript. Below: Illumination depicting crusaders

man might make his fortune in plunder or land.

Sir Edmund, however, like *Joseph*, had had a dream. A friar passing through Lampwich had interpreted this dream as a message from God telling Sir Edmund that he would win everlasting forgiveness for his sins if he journeyed to Outremer. Sir Edmund's protest that no one went on Crusades any more was brushed aside by the friar who told him that he should go alone if necessary.

Sir Edmund was unusually devout for a knight and decided that he must go. Money had been a problem. He had even had to sell off some of his land to his villeins and rent more to tenants in order to raise the money for a strong *destrier* and packhorses. Then there had been the crippling expense of new armour, for the suit he had worn at *Crécy* had rusted badly. William Palmer had been given the job of cleaning it and when he had finished swirling it about in a huge barrel containing the usual mixture of sand and vinegar it had gleamed like new; but there were places where it did not gleam – no steel was left. The holes would give easy passage to a Saracen sword and Sir Edmund, journeying through Europe, would have been a laughing-stock. So he had had to buy a new suit of armour.

28

Above: Illustration from a French medieval manuscript showing the English King, Edward III, wounding Philip VI, King of France, at the battle of Crécy in 1346, at which the English were victorious. **Left:** From a later English manuscript, Christians riding off to the Crusades against the Saracens in the Holy Land

Above: Two young ladies of the 14th century.
Below: Impression of Bristol Castle as seen in
1480. Built shortly after the Norman Conquest,
it was still in full use in 1370, and was under the
King's control as confirmed by the Royal Bristol
Charter of 1373

His bride of three months, the fourteen-year-old Lady
Anne, bore the news of his departure for the Holy Land
without distress. Her parents had arranged her marriage
to this forty-five-year-old knight despite her protests that
she wanted a far younger man. They had not even managed
to be business-like about the affair. For her husband had
had to sell land, tell her that she might have little money for
fine clothes and that it was her duty to manage the estate –
or what remained of it – until he returned, having won a
clear conscience for the rest of his days.

Jack of Newbury realised that his own visit and wares
were a small matter compared with the drama of the
return of the lord of the manor. Some bad news would
bring their attention back to him.

'Have you the *plague* here?' he asked of the nearest
woman. Very quickly the talk of Sir Edmund died away
and there was a silence. In the following instants memories
passed through all their minds of the terrible days when the
Black Death had raged in their village for month after
month, taking the young and old, the poor and well-to-do,
and whole families. Some had awoken in their full strength,
eaten a hearty dinner at 11 o'clock and been dead by
supper at 5 o'clock in the evening.

After it had raged for seven months there were fifty

30

people left alive in a Lampwich where two hundred had lived. Many houses were empty, the fields could not be cared for, and much of the livestock had to be killed off and salted. Since that time over twenty years before, the plague had not returned to Lampwich but travelling merchants, tinkers, pedlars and friars had sometimes passed through with stories of the Black Death appearing again, raging in other lands and in parts of England too. Jack had his audience again and the affairs of the manor were forgotten.

Meg Palmer broke the silence and asked him why he spoke of the plague; the rest of the women waited, listening for a kind of sentence of death. Jack smiled to himself inwardly. As far as he knew there was no plague in England that year. Quickly he told them that he had heard stories of a ship bringing wine from Bordeaux, that had arrived in Bristol with a case of the plague on board. He had not heard that the disease was spreading, he said, and had asked the women only to reassure himself. The women relaxed. Bristol was many many miles away and, although the plague could spread very rapidly indeed, no other traveller had brought news to bring them any fear. They now felt a kind of gratitude towards Jack, as if he were a bringer of good news and soon his trade became brisk. There was more money about in the years following the plague. With so few men to work the fields, wages had doubled even though laws had been made to set them back as they were before the plague.

Although his customers had coin in their purses, as he expected, there were no buyers for his pewter and brightly coloured cloth. These families lived with a single metal cup to a household, and the more expensive bright linens and woollens were not for them either. But his trade was brisk in pins, needles, cheap pottery of designs not made in the village, and coarse lengths of linen that were near-canvas from which they would make smocks, tunics, loose gowns and bed-coverings. He had remedies too for coughs, headaches, fever, pregnancy, smallpox, the curse of a witch and even the plague itself. Despite the fear his news had brought them there were few buyers for this. They all remembered how the many potions, prayers and tears had done no good whatsoever.

Above: A pottery jug of the 13th century. **Below:** A man with an axe and hunting horn, wearing a tunic, a smock and a wide-brimmed hat on his head

31

Two hunting scenes from medieval illuminated manuscripts. Notice that the size of the characters is determined by their importance rather than by realistic perspective

Eventually the buying was done and it was time for him to move on to a better market. He had heard enough about the manor and the people who lived and worked there to know that he could gain admittance – perhaps to the Lady Anne herself, who might want some of his bright linen for a new gown for the night's feast.

Although it had been a rushed affair, the hunt gathered in the manor courtyard was still a vivid sight. There had not been time to invite many important people, but those who had come had brought with them *retainers* so that about forty were ready to take part. Abbot Hubert was looking forward to the chase more than most. He knew that hunting was not a proper activity for a man of God, and in the first place he had taken it up so that it gave him the opportunity to mix easily with the people he had Abbey business with. If you had hunted with a merchant, he was more likely to give you the price you asked for a crop of oats without too much quibbling. It was much the same as regards a knight who held land of the Abbey and was behind with his rent – far easier to remind the gentleman of the fact after a good day's hunting. However, today he could see nothing to concern himself about other than the thrill of the chase. The dogs looked a good set and should ensure that there was good sport, and the huntsman, William Palmer, looked the kind of fellow who would set a sensible pace and make sure that the ground was not too difficult. The Abbot liked a good brisk ride but was not eager to break his neck in a wild headlong chase.

Tom was feeling nervous. It was the first time he had taken part in a hunt with the responsibility of falconer. His peregrines were trained well enough for flights near the manor but they might not be so obedient on strange ground nor with so many more people about.

Sir Edmund had a headache. He would have much preferred to stay in bed at least until it was time for the feasting to begin, but of course he had to do his duty to his guests. That pot-bellied Sir Walter d'Anville would guffaw all over him if he had pleaded a headache and stayed at the manor.

William, like Tom, was nervous but felt that he could manage the hunt quite adequately. He would lead them off at a fast gallop along the water meadows and then up the rise to a beech wood. They might pick up the scent of a hare in the meadows or a stag in the wood. There were thickets there too where wild boar might be lurking. Once they came across a scent his task would really be over. Everyone would make off pell-mell or more cautiously, depending on their enthusiasm; then it would be up to him to collect any stragglers and perhaps to see that anyone who was unhorsed was not seriously injured.

The Lady Anne watched, restraining a yawn. There had been gossip about the hunting she had done while Sir Edmund was away and she had thought it best to say to Sir Edmund that she had little taste for the sport now. She would stay behind and supervise arrangements for the feast. Sir Edmund had nodded his approval of such good sense in a young head.

Jack of Newbury watched too as the hunt set out. It seemed that he might be in luck. Obviously the feast had

Stripping the boar after the hunt, part of an early manuscript with decorated initial letters and margins. Notice the men preparing vegetables in the foreground and the hunting dogs around the fire

33

Above: Medieval kitchen scene showing large open fireplace. **Right:** Cooks roasting meat on a spit, turned by hand by a kitchen boy. The size of the basting spoon has been exaggerated

A bronze cooking vessel of the 14th century

been hurriedly arranged. He might find that there was a need for a few pieces of pewterware for the tables tonight or, even better, the Lady Anne might be persuaded into buying some of his expensive cloth for a gown. She could not have had much need of fine clothes during the past few years.

He decided to approach her as she turned back towards the manor.

EVENING

The kitchen at the manor was very large indeed. Although Sir Edmund was not fond of entertaining and did as little as possible, the room itself had been built before his time on a grand scale, and it measured nearly forty feet across. The *master mason* responsible for its construction had borne it in mind that many people would have to work there when a banquet was being prepared. Kitchens were often constructed as separate buildings and were connected to the Great Hall, where the guests would eat, by a covered corridor. This arrangement cut down the risk of a manor or castle burning down if fire broke out in the kitchen, which often happened in medieval times.

Meg Palmer looked around her, pausing for a moment to wipe the sweat from her brow. She was one of thirty there, and despite its size the room seemed crowded. Set into two of the walls were vast open fireplaces over which two young lads were slowly turning spits which rested on two cast-iron, V-shaped forks. On one spit was a whole ox and the lad was having a difficult task to crank its sizzling bulk above the flames. That an ox had been killed for the feast showed it was an occasion of importance, for these animals were essential for pulling the ploughs and carts that kept the manor going. On the other spit there were two sheep carcasses. There was other meat being prepared as well in huge metal cauldrons. Some of these stood directly in the flames on their three short legs, while others were hung above the fire from a hook and chain with a device that allowed the cauldron to be raised and lowered according to how much heat was needed in the cooking. These huge pots contained stews of various kinds of meats – beef, hares that Tom's peregrines had taken that afternoon, a wild boar that Sir Edmund had speared in the brushwood shortly after, and joints of pork and poultry too. Many spices had been used in the preparation because people liked their food to be peppery and to have a strong flavour. This taste had resulted largely from the slaughter of animals in the autumn; long before the following spring much of the meat would be in poor condition or even maggot-ridden and rotten. Spices helped to conceal this.

Meg was busy preparing the vegetables which were also added to the stews. At present she was chopping very strong-scented onions and garlic so her eyes ran with tears. When she had completed this task she would move on to washing the fruit that would be served towards the end of the banquet.

There were not many kitchen utensils to be seen. The chief cook was using a *cleaver* and needed to be the strong man he was in order to split through carcasses with an untiring right arm. There were many knives in use, cutting, slicing and chopping, and over one of the cauldrons a large *flesh hook* was in use. This was a long metal prong set in a wooden handle with three more prongs sticking out from its sides. Just now it was being used to grip joints of meat in the pot in order to turn them and check them to see if they were ready. It was also used for heaving the cooked joints from the pot and on to the silver platters on which they would be served later. They would lie in the hearths in the meantime.

Meg's next-door neighbour was labouring with a *mortar* and *pestle*, grinding and mixing the spices for a sauce. The ingredients she was using were ginger, cinnamon, saffron, garlic, cloves and pepper and she would later add *verjuice*,

Above: A bronze cooking pot of the 14th century

Below: (right) a cleaver used for cutting large joints of meat and (left) a flesh hook

35

A bronze mortar, 3 inches in height

onions, wine and vinegar to the saucepan in which it would be prepared.

As the pace of the work increased some of the people working there – particularly the chief cook – began to get more ill-tempered and there was much swearing and threatening. It seemed that the guests had gathered in the Great Hall and that the meal was late. At last the early meat courses were ready and the servers were organized into a line so that the procession could lead out of the kitchen and along the covered way to the hall.

In the Great Hall the guests were not at all impatient. Most of them were pleasantly tired after the afternoon's hunting and the time was passing agreeably enough in listening to the harpists and lute players.

The various tables had been set out around the hall. The high table at which Sir Edmund and his honoured guests were sitting was a glittering sight. Here were gathered the best items of his tableware: silver plates and cups and spoons. The guests would use their own knives which they wore at their waists; forks were hardly known in England.

Above: Procession of servants about to enter the banqueting hall. **Right:** A 16th century mazer bowl, similar to the type used in medieval manor houses

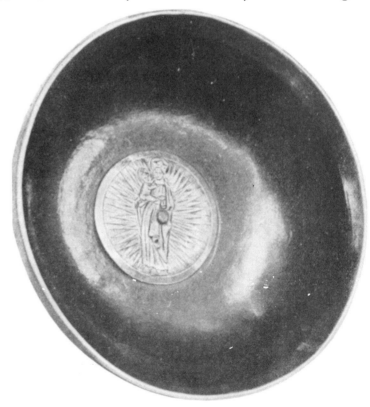

36

Instead people used their fingers and washed them in finger bowls now and then. Perhaps the chief ornament on the high table was the great salt-cellar which only the lord of the house used, though he might also choose to serve others from it; each one of the guests had a less magnificent salt-cellar for his own use. There was one plate between two people, and a knight and lady, for example, would share the food from it and would also use one wine cup between them. Most of the cups were silver but there were some *mazers* in use as well. These were cups made from the finest grained maple-wood, with a silver lid and fine silver decorations around the sides and at the base.

An iron candlestick

The high table was lit by wax candles – for such an important occasion Sir Edmund had felt it was worth the extra cost. Guests on the other tables had to make do with burning bundles of rushes which had been soaked in fat. These were generally placed on the walls, and as they gave a rather dim and smoky light the less important guests were not going to find it too easy to see what food they were eating.

By now the procession had reached the Great Hall from the kitchens and, after the journey down the draughty corridor and the time taken in the kitchen to check that everything was in order, the food was no longer hot; but no one minded this. The piquancy of the spices made it quite difficult anyway to tell if the food was hot or cold. At the head of the procession the bearer of the great wine cup approached the high table and the cup was passed from one guest to another. Later the individual goblets would be used.

A bronze pricket candle-holder

Everyone was now seated except for those serving food and drink. Tom, in recompense for his successes as falconer that day had been entrusted with the task of serving Abbot Hubert. The Abbot watched his clumsiness with some amusement, and the manners of fellow guests with distaste. All of them, including even the Lady Anne, were eating greedily and were not troubling at the sauces and juices that ran down from their mouths on to their fine clothes. Sir Edmund plunged his hand as deep as the wrist into a dish of stew to draw out a choice piece – and then he completely forgot his manners in not offering it to his wife.

37

Above: An English manor house built at the end of the 13th century.
Below: Beautifully decorated drinking horn of the 14th century, with birds' feet

The chicken leg eaten, he tossed the bone on the rush-covered floor without further thought; the dogs soon finished it off, snarling and nipping at each other in the hunger that followed their afternoon at the hunt.

Things were better ordered at St. Bartholomew's, thought Abbot Hubert. He expected his monks to eat carefully. They must not allow food to drop from their mouths on to the tablecloth or dribble down their chins. It was also forbidden to wipe the mouth with the back of the hand as Lady Anne was doing. And now here was Sir Edmund passing him the great wine cup with one hand only and slopping the wine over both the table and the Abbot's best robe. Hubert forced a smile of thanks to his lips, and waved away Sir Edmund's apologies. The man seemed to be drunk already, and at his own feast too. It would be an uphill task, thought Hubert, for English knights to learn good manners.

At the other tables everyone was eating well. Although

38

the dishes passed from table to table according to the order of importance of the guests, and the choicest pieces of meat were gone long before they reached the lowest table, there was sufficient for all. This was because so many dishes were served : there were six meat courses with about twenty dishes for each course. Even Sir Walter d'Anville, who had the reputation of a glutton, could not manage to eat a helping of all of them.

So the early hours of the evening – the meal had begun at five o'clock – passed in eating, drinking, talk, shouting and the snarling of dogs. The minstrel did his best and sang his songs of knightly love and adventure but it seemed that no one was interested. He decided to save his voice until later on when everyone had eaten enough, when those who were drunk would have fallen under the tables, and those who were still sober enough would have little energy left with their full stomachs and wine-fuddled heads to do anything other than sit and listen.

Impression of a banquet at the French Court in the 14th century. Notice the swan and the peacock being carried ceremonially to the table. It was customary in Court and manor house alike to allow dogs to be present at the feasts and to eat the scraps

39

Eventually the last course, called the *issue*, was served. This consisted of nuts and a variety of the fruits in season. Everyone enjoyed the freshness of the fruit after the richness of the sauces and the hotness of the spices. Then all the silver and earthenware plates were taken away and only the cups were left while the pitchers of wine continued to pass to and fro among the guests.

Sir Edmund felt that it had been a good home-coming. On his campaign in the East and in prison, he had unwillingly become used to eating no more than did the poorest of his own cottars. The feast had been a treat which he was sure he well deserved. Mellow with food and drink he listened approvingly as the minstrel sang a ballad which told of brave knights leaving all they most loved behind them, and venturing far across the seas on Crusade. The minstrel too was pleased when Sir Edmund fumbled in the pouch at his waist and flung him a silver penny.

The Lady Anne was becoming very bored. She had paid little attention to the minstrel's songs during the feasting. Her attention then had been on Sir Edmund's squire Robert who, as he had served her with food and drink, had also given her a great many looks showing great devotion.

Above: Fragment of a popular German poem of the 13th century, showing the musical notation of the period. **Below:** A 14th century pitcher with a yellow glaze and decoration of stripes and scales. **Right:** The squire, an illustration from Chaucer's 'Canterbury Tales', written c. 1387

THE SQUIRE.

40

She wished now that the minstrel would sing a ballad of love and the devotion of gallant knights, though it seemed she would have to make do with a squire.

Jack of Newbury had drunk little during the feast. He wanted to keep a clear head and his eyes open for the chance of a sale. When the platters had been cleared away he had watched William Palmer and waited for an opportunity to move over near him. No one would mind at this stage in the evening. Before the hunt he had noticed that William's leather gauntlets were worn through at the palm. Jack had bought far too many a few months before, though at a cheap price, and was always on the look-out for a sale. He moved to William's table and after some idle talk managed to lead the conversation to the price of leather. In a short time a price was agreed.

Abbot Hubert was the first to leave. He would have liked to have made the journey back to St. Bartholomew's that night but because of thieves and other rogues it was not really safe to travel at night even though he had his men-at-arms as escort. He now withdrew to his room. The talk was becoming unfit for the ears of a churchman, and the other guests would prefer to talk more freely without his presence.

Above left: From a 13th century manuscript, Adenez 'the King of the Minstrels' entertains the Queen of France. **Above:** 'Summer is i-cumen in', a famous round of the late 13th century. **Below:** An all too frequent occurrence on the streets at night

41

The pace of the evening had now slowed down. The minstrel sang quiet mournful songs and nearly everyone drank deeply. All hunger was satisfied and even the dogs had full bellies.

At last Sir Edmund rose to his feet unsteadily. It was the signal that the feasting was over. Those who had sat at high table walked or were helped to the rooms allotted to them – in most cases they were sharing, and even Sir Edmund and the Lady Anne did not sleep alone, though they had the privacy of curtaining around the bed. The common folk made their way back to the village or stretched themselves out on the benches in the Great Hall. For them especially, it had been a day that would long be remembered.

42

Glossary

Archbishop of Canterbury	head of the church in England
bailiff	the lord of the manor's agent
barter	to buy and sell by exchanging goods
Benedictine	order of monks founded by St. Benedict
Black Death	a devastating plague that killed about one third of the people in the countries affected
bordar	a very poor peasant
cleaver	hatchet-like tool for chopping meat
cloisters	covered walk, usually walled on one side, with a colonnade facing the quadrangle on the other side
cottars	poor peasants occupying a cottage
coverts	thickets frequented by game
Crécy	famous battle of 1346 fought in France, in which Edward III of England defeated Philip VI of France
Crusade	expedition to reclaim the Holy Land from the Mohammedans
delve	dig
demesne	estate
destrier	a war-horse
doublet	close-fitting article of clothing (similar to a jacket) worn by men
falconer	a man who trains hawks and hunts with them
fallow	a field left unused for the land to recover fertility
fiefs	estates
flesh hook	tool used to move hot meat
furlong	an eighth of a mile; the word comes from the Anglo Saxon, 'furlang', meaning 'the length of a furrow'
germinate	to produce shoots or buds
glebe	land belonging to the village clergy
groat	silver coin in use between 1351–1662, worth about 2p
hair shirt	under garment made of rough, itchy material
Henry II	King of England 1154–1189
heriot	a tax, the best animal in the possession of a villein was taken by the lord on the villein's death
hose	stockings
issue	course of fruit and nuts served at the end of a banquet
Joseph	Jacob's son, the dreamer (see the Bible, Book of Genesis)
kerchiefs	piece of cloth to cover the head
Lauds	second service of the day, recited at sunrise, but now often joined with Matins
mason	a man skilled in the use of stone
master mason	chief builder, the architect of medieval times
Matins	the first service of the day, recited or sung at midnight
mazer	a drinking bowl mounted in silver and made from a hard wood, usually maple
merchant	trader
merchet	tax paid to a lord of the manor when a villein's daughter married
Monte Cassino	hill in Italy
mortar	a vessel of hard material used for pounding and mixing with a pestle
Moslem	a follower of the prophet Mohammed
mummers	travelling players; as church services were in Latin, the performances of plays given by the mummers were the only contact people had with the Bible in the English language
Outremer	literally 'beyond the seas', it meant the countries in which the Crusades were fought

43

pallet	a straw bed
panniers	large baskets for carrying goods, often carried by a donkey
pardoner	a man who was licensed to sell to the people pardons for their sins
pedlar	travelling seller of cheap goods
peregrine	kind of falcon, much prized for hunting
pestle	club-shaped implement for pounding substances in a mortar
Peter of Cyprus	leader of one of the last Crusades – a very minor one
pig in a poke	'poke' means 'sack'; to buy a pig in a poke means to get a bad bargain, not having inspected the goods beforehand
plague	an epidemic disease, such as the Black Death
ransom	money demanded for the release of someone
reeve	person elected to act as a middleman between the village and the manor
retainers	dependants or servants of a lord or knight
St. Thomas à Becket	Henry II's Chancellor and later Archbishop of Canterbury; murdered in Canterbury Cathedral
Saracens	at this time the word meant Arabs or Moslems
scriptorium	room set aside for the purpose of writing, particularly in a monastery
selective breeding	choosing the best animals to breed from
squire	a knight's attendant
tonsure	shaven area of a monk's head
verjuice	juice of unripe grapes, apples or crab-apples. Often used instead of vinegar
vetches	plants of the pea family fed to animals
villeins	feudal serfs, although not at the poorest level of society

44

General Notes

WARFARE IN THE MIDDLE AGES

Although our century has seen Britain involved in the two most terrible wars of our history, and in several others that have mainly been the concern of our professional fighting men, this has still been a century during which we have been at peace for many of its years. If we go back only as far as **Victorian** times we find that every year, almost without an exception, saw British soldiers at war. Sometimes these were major conflicts but usually they were minor ones in connection with our **Empire.**

In the **Middle Ages** there was no Empire, no defined Britain; the wars were English. **Edward I** completed a conquest of Wales and brought back a weapon that was shortly to make the English army the most feared on the continent of Europe. It was a weapon the origins of which go back to times before there was any written history – the bow and arrow. Used by prehistoric man mainly for hunting, but no doubt in tribal and group fighting as well, it became less important until reaching a new dominance on battle-fields during the reign of **Edward III**, the time this book refers to.

For many years English kings were ambitious, not so much to found an empire stretching far across the seas – they knew little or nothing of Africa, India, China and the Americas – but to make the mainland into one kingdom. They wished to regain and enlarge the provinces of **France** held by the first **Norman** kings and, if possible, to include the whole of France in their kingdom. There were frequent wars with **Scotland**, mainly fought in the north of England and the south of Scotland. **Neville's Cross** was an important victory won by **Edward III's** queen in 1346. The same year saw the battle of **Crécy**, one of the most complete English victories over the French of the **Hundred Years' War,** which continued on and off from 1338–1453. In 1356 came the battle of **Poitiers.** Together with **Agincourt,** these were the main English victories in the successive attempts of English kings to enlarge their possessions across the Channel or to gain the throne of France. Almost all were won with the aid of the **long-bow.** The nobles of France persisted in seeing war as a man-to-man conflict between heavily armoured mounted **knights** trying – but not often succeeding – to hack each other to death. The **archers** of the English armies kept their distance from this kind of combat and shot down the knights from convenient vantage points. Although ideas of knightly **chivalry** and the presence of knights on the battlefield continued for some time yet, the five-foot-long English long-bow, with its superior range and speed of reloading, had made the **cross-bow** almost obsolete.

TRADE AND COMMERCE

Today our shops and homes contain manufactured goods and products from many countries of the world. Tinned goods, for example, come from the Argentine, France, the United States, China, Poland, Italy, Australia, South Africa, Israel and the Arab countries, to name but a few.

It was very different in the fourteenth century. The typical English villager would not think of buying anything at all for most of the year. He ate what he grew and sold any surplus produce of a good year. Much of what he wore and the simple tools he used to farm his land were made in his own home. If he had any money saved, he would buy from a travelling pedlar or merchant on the rare occasions that one visited his village.

Things were somewhat different in the towns, for some shops did exist, and craftsmen sold their wares in these and on the streets. Despite this, the range of things that could be bought was quite limited.

Powerful monasteries had accumulated much wealth from their large holdings in land and their control of small-scale industries, but at this time the real economy of England was founded on the **wool trade.** Nearly all the income from overseas came from the export of raw wool and, later on, of finished cloth as well. It was the wealth of the monasteries and the profits of the wool trade that helped to build the medieval churches of England.

EDUCATION IN MEDIEVAL TIMES

Education to an ordinary English villager of the fourteenth century meant whatever the village **parson** chose to teach him. The parson should not be confused with the often learned **monks** of the monasteries of England. He usually knew enough **Latin** to carry through a church service in the language, and could teach the villagers in his care very little besides the **moral teachings** of the Christian religion, stories of Christ's life, and other tales drawn from the **Old Testament.**

Popular education was not in fact thought highly of. Very few, if any, would have argued that all English people should be able to read and write, or know more than simple arithmetic. It would have been thought dangerous for the ordinary townsman and villager to have a little learning, as he might not be content with his lowly way of life and position in society. However, the **knightly classes** were themselves little interested in what we now consider education. If a young **squire** were being 'educated' at a nobleman's house, he would be taught only the accomplishments necessary to a knight. He would learn how to handle a horse and a variety of weapons, how to serve at table, to

45

prepare his lord's armour, and the behaviour expected of a knight in both peace and war. He might also hear a few of the popular songs of the day, which mainly concerned knightly deeds of valour and romantic love.

The people with anything approaching an education in the modern sense were those who chose to become monks, or those who went to the universities of **Oxford** and **Cambridge,** both of which had been in existence for more than a hundred years. The subjects studied in both the monasteries and the universities were limited though. One learned more about the Bible and the language in which it was written – Latin – than anything else. Those that had advanced further might study **theology** and **philosophy**, for which Oxford was renowned throughout Europe. Scholars who wished to study mathematics, for example, had to travel far to find a teacher, or, in these days before printing, the necessary books.

Those that became educated might choose the life of the monastery or university or, if ambitious for worldly success, seek service with nobles. Of those who served the king, only a few rose to influential positions as a result of their education.

ENGLISH LANGUAGE AND LITERATURE

Modern English is a development from the mixture of many languages, resulting from invasions of Britain, and the movements of peoples through the centuries.

At the middle of the fourteenth century, the **French language** was not as important as is often thought. In the centuries immediately after the **Norman Conquest** it was, of course, the language of the king's court and of nobles, and was used in the courts of law. By the middle of the fourteenth century English was replacing it. By this time many French words had come into the English language and have remained: farm, beef, mutton, peasant, and many, many more.

Whereas today **travel and communications** have encouraged the development of a standard language, in medieval times this was not the case. **Dialects** varied even between neighbouring villages and, in fact, people from different parts of the country may hardly have been able to understand one another at all.

Broadly speaking, however, there were three main dialects: **Northern, Southern** and **Kentish and Midland.** As the Northern lost 'unnecessary' endings to nouns, adjectives and verbs the most quickly, a piece of Northern literature looks more familiar to the modern reader than does the language **Chaucer** wrote. The Midlands contained the two most important universities and the capital, **London.** As all capitals are, amongst other things, meeting places, the Midland dialect gradually became the one that dominated the others.

Latin was the international language of the time. Scholars and churchmen all over Europe could write or speak in that language, but it was solely the language of the educated, of scholars and monks, not of workers, nor even of knights and their ladies, who were mostly illiterate.

By the middle of the fourteenth century, however, English as a language had at last regained the position it had lost at the Norman Conquest. It became increasingly more popular as the language of literature. Two of the first great writers of the English language were **Geoffrey Chaucer** and **William Langland**, while **John Wycliffe** translated the Bible into English. Langland's most famous work was **'Piers the Ploughman'** which, while championing the cause of the poor, also ridicules much of contemporary society. Chaucer is regarded as the founder of modern English literature although he was very much influenced by the leading French and Italian writers of his day. His most well-known works are **'Troilus and Criseyde',** and, of course, the **'Canterbury Tales'.** Both of these were written about twenty years after the time to which this book refers.

46

Index

Abbey, 7, 8, 9, 32
Abbot, 7, 8, 32, 37, 38
Agriculture, 8, 11, 12, 13, 14, 15, 16, 18, 19
Archbishop of Canterbury, 9

Bailiff, 15, 16
Benedictine, 7
Black Death, 11, 12, 30, 31
Bordar, 16
Bordeaux, 31
Bristol, 8, 31

Celebrations, 15, 36–42
Cleaver, 35
Clothing, 24, 25, 27
Cottars, 8, 16
Coverts, 9
Crécy, 28
Crops, 12, 13, 18, 19
Crusades, 9, 11, 15, 19, 21, 27, 28, 30

Demesne, 19
Doublet, 24

Exeter, 8

Falconer, 16, 22, 33
Feast, 15, 16, 22, 36, 37, 38, 39, 40, 41, 42
Flesh hook, 35
Food, 22, 34, 35, 36, 37, 38, 39, 40
Furniture, 7, 8

Glebe, 19
Groat, 15

Henry II, 9
Heriot, 13
Holy Land, 9, 15, 21, 30
Hose, 24, 25, 27
Hunting, 9, 15, 16, 22, 32, 33

Jerusalem, 15, 27
Joseph, 28

Kerchief, 25, 27
Kitchen utensils, 35

Lands, 7
London, 8

Manor house, 8, 34
Matins, 7
Mazer, 37
Merchet, 13
Minstrel, 39, 41, 42
Monte Cassino, 7
Mortar, 35
Moslem, 27
Mummers, 15

Outremer, 21, 27, 28

Palestine, 27
Pallet, 7
Pardoner, 9
Pedlars' wares, 17, 24, 25, 27, 31
Peregrine, 16, 22, 33
Pestle, 35
Peter of Cyprus, crusade of, 11
Plague, 11, 12, 30, 31
Pope, 27

Reeve, 11, 22
Religion, 7, 8, 9

St. Benedict, 8
St. Thomas à Becket, 9
Saracens, 13, 14, 27, 28
Scriptorium, 7
Syria, 21, 27

Taxes, 13

Villeins, 8, 11, 13, 28

Further Reading

An Age of Ambition   F. R. H. du Boulay (Nelson, 1969)

The Medieval Foundation   Arthur Bryant (Collins, 1966)

English Costume   Dion Clayton Calthrop (A. & C. Black, 1907)

Chaucer and his England   G. G. Coulton (Methuen, 1965)

Life in the Middle Ages   G. G. Coulton (Cambridge University Press, 1968)

The Black Death and the Peasants' Revolt   Leonard W. Cowie (Wayland, 1972)

The Making of Britain: Life and Work to the Close of the Middle Ages   T. K. Derry and M. G. Blakeway (Murray, 1968)

The Peasants' Revolt   *Ed.* R. B. Dobson (Macmillan, 1970)

The Fourteenth Century   May McKisack (Oxford University Press, 1959)

Roman and Medieval Britain   W. P. D. Murphy (Nelson, 1969)

The Great Revolt of 1381   Sir Charles Oman (Oxford University Press, 1969)

A History of Everyday Things in England, Vol. I   Marjorie and C. H. B. Quennel (Batsford, 1957)

Illustrated English Social History, Vol. I   Sir G. M. Trevelyan (Longmans, 1969)

We hope you have enjoyed this book and will go on to find out more about the period.

If your favourite subject in history has not been included so far, then the Editors would be delighted to hear from you. Write to us at the following address and we shall be pleased to consider your suggestion for a book later in the series:

The Editors (Day Books)
Robert Tyndall Ltd.,
45 Grand Parade,
Brighton BN2 2QA,
Sussex, England